THEN & NOW

LEE COUNTY

OPPOSITE: This 1940s photograph was taken in the section of Fort Myers known as Safety Hill. During the segregation years of 1876–1965, the Jim Crow laws in Fort Myers forbade any African American from crossing the railroad tracks after dark. As a result, the community of Safety Hill was established. Some believe the area's name is derived from the security it emanated. Despite segregation, the community thrived and contributed to the growth and success of Lee County. Today Safety Hill is commonly recognized as Dunbar. (Photograph courtesy of Southwest Florida Museum of History.)

THEN & NOW

LEE COUNTY

Kim Phillips

This book is lovingly dedicated to the memory of my father, Edward M. Phillips, from whom I've inherited my passion for the past.

ISBN 978-0-7385-8703-6

Library of Congress Control Number: 2010931587

Published by Arcadia Publishing
Charleston, South Carolina

Printed in the United States of America

For all general information, please contact Arcadia Publishing:
Telephone 843-853-2070
Fax 843-853-0044
E-mail sales@arcadiapublishing.com
For customer service and orders:
Toll-Free 1-888-313-2665

Visit us on the Internet at www.arcadiapublishing.com

On the Front Cover: Cut off from the mainland, early travelers between Pine Island and Fort Myers would have to journey by wagon to St. James City and then board a steamer for Fort Myers. In 1927, Harry Stringfellow and Bruce Scott finally convinced Lee County to erect a bridge over Matlacha Pass. The original wooden bridge was replaced in 1968. The new concrete bridge is 10 feet wider, accommodates two lanes of traffic, and provides a catwalk for local fishermen. (Photograph courtesy of Southwest Florida Museum of History and Kim Phillips.)

On the Back Cover: This 1930 photograph shows the last remaining fort building of the Third Seminole War and U.S. Civil War at Fort Myers. Serving as the commanding officer's quarters, its original location was the corner of First and Jackson Streets. After many renovations, and just as many owners, the house was moved to its Bay Street location in 1926 to serve as Fort Myer's first public library. It was torn down in 1937. (Photograph courtesy of Southwest Florida Museum of History.)

Contents

Acknowledgments

First and foremost, I would like to thank Lindsay Harris of Arcadia Publishing for your encouragement and guidance through this process.

I would like to thank the following guardians of the past whose contributions were invaluable to this publication: Pamela Miner and Victor Zarick of the Southwest Florida Museum of History for opening your archives to me; Genevieve and Peter Bowen, Helen Ferrell, Sara Nell Gran, Pat Jungferman, and Gerri Reaves of the Southwest Florida Historical Society, all Fort Myers icons who tirelessly rendered assistance and shared their recollections of early Fort Myers and Lee County; Gina Taylor of the Lee Trust for Historic Preservation for pointing me in the right direction; Michele Hylton of the Fort Myers Redevelopment Agency for your help in trying to locate original photographs; Anne C. Cull and Pat Molter of the Cape Coral Historical Society Museum for sharing your expertise and family history with me; Kim Kyle of the Boca Grande Historical Society for your expertise on Boca Grande's history; James White of Alva who befriended me on Pearl Street, proudly sharing the history of Alva, patiently answering my questions, and pointing me in the right direction; the wonderful ladies at the Alva Museum for sharing their knowledge of the history of Alva; the Captiva Memorial librarian who chose to remain nameless, yet held nothing back when it came to sharing her expertise on Sanibel and Captiva.

Those who must never be forgotten are the early Lee County pioneers. The intrepid souls, who most times with nothing but a dream in their heart, bravely carved the county we know today out of a swamped, mangled wilderness.

Last but never least, I would to thank my family, my friends, and my trusty sidekick for your love, support, and patience as I worked on this project.

Introduction

In studying the history of an area, sometimes we tend to focus on what remains, those things we can hold in our hands. It can easily escape us that once there were people, places, and things we can no longer see.

In writing this book, I have tried to maintain a balance of what is still here and what is not. Many of my modern-day photographs are of nondescript empty fields, service stations, and paved highways; however, that is where the history happened. People who approached me as I took pictures for this book were astonished at what was once right beneath their feet. Some were shocked to learn that Cape Coral had a history before it was Cape Coral, or of the vanished communities of Punta Rassa and Slater.

It is wonderful to visit museums, historic sites, and estate homes. These beautiful places promote education and historic preservation, but the majority of these notable sites are rarely restored and hardly protected. In many cases, the records of locations and dates are long lost, if ever recorded at all. Every place has a history that theoretically can be traced back to the beginning of time. It is this forgotten history that is usually the most interesting.

My goal in comparing photographs of old Lee County to the landscape of today is to generate that zeal for recognizing the past in the present.

All modern photographs were provided by the author unless specified otherwise.

CHAPTER 1

THE EARLY YEARS

Survey, the original name for Bonita Springs, derived from the survey crews sent to map the area. Their camp was located on the southern bank of what is now the Imperial River, near a spring that natives claimed had healing powers. In the late 1880s, pioneers began moving into the abandoned survey camps; thus, dubbing their new community "Survey." (Photograph courtesy of Southwest Florida Museum of History.)

Long gone is the date palm Capt. Winfield Scott Hancock planted at the corner of First and Jackson Streets in commemoration of the birth of his daughter in 1857. At the time, the captain was serving as the quartermaster for Fort Myers. Later, as a general, Hancock would distinguish himself in the U.S. Civil War and as a presidential candidate. This 1927 photograph is a stark contrast to today's scenery outside of the Sidney and Berne Davis Art Center. (Photograph courtesy of Southwest Florida Museum of History.)

The origin of Bonita Springs stems from a tiny spring that still flows into Oak Creek today. Gilmer Heitman purchased the property and built the Bonita Springs Hotel in 1924. Believing the springwater contained healing properties, Dr. Charles Gnau purchased the hotel and spring in the 1960s. The following owner, R. J. Cheatham, renamed the hotel the Shangri-La Resort and offered luxurious spa treatments to upscale clientele. There were discussions to bottle the springwater, but plans were never finalized. (Photograph courtesy of Southwest Florida Historical Society.)

To keep up with the growing population of Estero, the Estero Land Company was set up in Key West to sell plots to potential residents in the area. In the earlier photograph, land is being cleared on the Estero River to make way for new settlers. It was also around this time that citrus growers discovered the area as a good investment for their groves. Today modern housing developments can be found along the banks of the Estero River. (Photograph courtesy of Southwest Florida Museum of History.)

The cottage seen above was built in 1882 by German immigrant Gustav Damkohler. Damkohler was the first settler of Estero, homesteading 160 acres of land. When Cyrus Teed moved his Koreshan Unity to Estero in 1894, Damkohler was impressed with the religion and donated a large tract of his land on the Estero River to the settlement. Damkohler's cottage, the only standing structure at the time, was used for living and dining until the Koreshans' new buildings were constructed. (Photograph courtesy of Southwest Florida Museum of History.)

This pre-1903 photograph shows the first general store and ferry landing at Alva, located on the Caloosahatchee River on the west side of Broadway Street at Pearl Street. Built by John and James English, the store was operated by Hugh Sampson. The construction of the steel swing bridge in 1903 eliminated the need for the ferry crossing, but the dock was kept in use. A real estate office now occupies the site. (Photograph courtesy of Southwest Florida Museum of History.)

First settled in the 1880s, the popularity of Estero quickly spread. The original town was centered on Old County Road, which eventually became U.S. Route 41, and the parallel Frantz Avenue, which is now known as Highland Avenue. The photograph at left illustrates the dangers and difficulties of traveling in the city during the 1920s. Old Country Road is now paved and leads to the modern, busy U.S. Route 41 of today between Estero and Fort Myers. (Photograph courtesy of Southwest Florida Museum of History.)

Established in Estero during 1894, Dr. Cyrus Teed's Koreshan Unity was a religious, celibate, and communal society. Pictured above is the Koreshan Planetary Court. Built in 1904, the three-story building housed the seven women who served on the Planetary Chamber, which was the governing council of the Koreshan Unity. The entire area is now preserved and maintained by the State of Florida as the Koreshan State Historic Site. (Photograph courtesy of Southwest Florida Museum of History.)

The isolation and hardships of the early island pioneers created a need for religious support and worship. In the above photograph is the Captiva Schoolhouse, which also served as the community church. Built in 1901, the building was sold to a Methodist conference in 1921 and renamed the Wayside Chapel. The Methodist religion was not very popular on Captiva Island, and in 1948, residents purchased the property back from the mission. The schoolhouse and church building was renovated and appropriately renamed Chapel by the Sea. (Photograph courtesy of Southwest Florida Museum of History.)

Pictured above is the second general store at the Koreshan Unity settlement. The first store faced the Estero River; however, with the opportunity provided by the new U.S. Route 41 in 1920, the Koreshan Unity built a new store facing the highway. The shop provided groceries, fishing supplies, and other basic staples of life not only to Koreshan members, but also to the entire community. The store officially closed its doors in 1963. (Photograph courtesy of Southwest Florida Museum of History.)

Although the building retains its original 1924 architecture, the Atlantic Coast Line Railroad Depot no longer resembles the railway station of yesterday. Long gone are the railroad tracks, ticket booths, and segregated black and white waiting rooms. Lush foliage now commands the landscape. The station was abandoned in 1971 but later renovated in 1982 to become the Fort Myers Historical Museum, today known as the Southwest Florida Museum of History. (Photograph courtesy of Southwest Florida Museum of History.)

Located at the intersection of Old U.S. Route 41 and Bonita Beach Road, this water tower portrays the rustic conditions that Bonita pioneers were forced to contend with. A modern gas station sits on the site today, providing a stark contrast between the modern world and Lee County's early years. In 1985, this tower was carefully dismantled and preserved. It was moved to Riverside Park, where it now stands on display. (Photograph courtesy of Southwest Florida Museum of History.)

The photograph below of the old Harney Point Road shows a region in early Cape Coral known as Heifer Heights. Cattle farming was a major industry in the fledgling community, with the Matlacha Cattle Company owning vast acreage. Cattle roaming free was a common sight in yesterday's Cape Coral. Today the Heifer Heights area boasts paved highways, stoplights, and lots of traffic. (Photograph courtesy of the Cape Coral Historical Society Museum.)

The Leitners were an early prominent Bonita family. When Keitte Leitner married Ada Bedell, they decided to make Bonita Springs their home. The Leitners successfully ran orange and grapefruit groves and even owned a freight boat. Seen below, the Leitner house was a kit home, transported by boat in pieces and assembled on East Terry Street, where it still stands. (Photograph courtesy of Southwest Florida Historical Society.)

Pilings are the only remainder of the once bustling wharf of old Punta Rassa today. The Sanibel Island Causeway Bridge provides the backdrop, rendering proof that the ferry is no longer needed. The area known as Punta Rassa figured prominently in Lee County's history. In 1837, during the Second Seminole War, the point was the site of Fort Dulaney. A hurricane destroyed the garrison in 1841, forcing commanders to relocate the fort. Punta Rassa is best known for its bustling cattle trade with Cuba. (Photograph courtesy of Southwest Florida Museum of History.)

After three requests dating back to 1833, Congress finally authorized the construction of the Sanibel Island Lighthouse in 1881. Sanibel's beacon was proudly shone for the first time on August 20, 1884. In 1972, the Coast Guard determined that the lighthouse was no longer necessary and would be shut down. Due to the public outcry, the Coast Guard abandoned its plan to extinguish the light. Today both the lighthouse and keeper's quarters are safely listed on the National Register of Historic Places. (Photograph courtesy of Southwest Florida Museum of History.)

When the International Ocean and Telegraph Company took over the old army barracks at Punta Rassa, Florida's wealthiest cattle baron, Jacob Summerlin, was forced to relocate his cattle operation a few hundred yards upriver. The Summerlin House was built in 1874 and used as living quarters for the cattlemen shipping their herds from Punta Rassa. By 1925, as the need for beef lessened and the railroads replaced cattle drives, most of the land in Punta Rassa was sold to Barron Collier. The Summerlin House was blown down in 1982. (Photograph courtesy of Southwest Florida Museum of History.)

Dean Park Historic District was the first real estate development for Fort Myers. Rhode Island furniture dealer John Morgan Dean purchased 38 acres of swampy land, which adjoined Billy's Creek. In 1910, Dean began the drainage and development process of the area. By 1914, the flooded lowlands were considered a prominent residential area. The 1920s photograph below shows one of the original Dean Park homes located on Providence Street. (Photograph courtesy of Southwest Florida Museum of History.)

CHAPTER 2

Playing Together, Praying Together

Originally named New Prospect, North Fort Myers provided three schools over the years; the above photograph shows the second. Although the second New Prospect School, this school was actually the first built and maintained by the Lee Board of Public Instruction. The original New Prospect School was built in 1887, the second in 1879, and the third in 1895. (Photograph courtesy of Southwest Florida Museum of History.)

The first schoolhouse in Fort Myers was believed to be this log cabin, built in 1873. Capt. F. A. Hendry was instrumental in the establishment of the school, hiring Englishman Robert Bell to serve as its first teacher. It is believed the site was located about where the annex of the Royal Palm Hotel was located. Other sources pinpoint the location down even further, approximately 100 yards downriver from the site of what was once the Hendry House, then the Royal Palm Hotel, followed by the Palmland, and eventually the Sheraton. (Photograph courtesy of Southwest Florida Museum of History.)

Sanibel Island's original Anglo-Saxon church, Dr. Barnes Church, was built in 1880 by the Reverend George O. Barnes of Kentucky. The reverend made sure the cross atop his church was visible to all sailors passing offshore. The final disposition of the church is unclear. Some sources claim the church was destroyed by a hurricane. Other sources contend the church was torn down to become a part of the cottages at "The Sisters," today's Casa Ybel Resort. (Photograph courtesy of Southwest Florida Historical Society.)

Early records are unclear if this 1910 photograph was of the first or second Survey School. Also unclear is the original site of the school pictured above; however, many sources agree it was located about where the Bonita Springs School was erected in 1921 and still stands today. This theory is based on the similarity of the descriptions of locations between the wooden school and the brick Bonita Springs School, given by those who attended. (Photograph courtesy of Southwest Florida Museum of History.)

Originally built in 1913 on the northern side of Anderson Avenue (now Martin Luther King Jr. Boulevard), the Williams Academy was the first government-funded school for black students in Lee County. It was moved to the Dunbar High School site on High Street in the 1930s. Today part of the original 1913 building serves as the Lee County Black History Society, located on Henderson Street. (Photograph courtesy of Southwest Florida Museum of History.)

Built in 1914, Alva High School was a community effort. Twenty-eight local residents all deeded portions of their own land for the school. The sand for the building's bricks came from the English family homestead and were fired by local men. Now Alva Elementary School, today's students study in classrooms that have remained quite similar to when their 1914 counterparts occupied them. The only visible change to the school building in the photograph below is the staircase on the side and the covered walkway. (Photograph courtesy of Southwest Florida Museum of History.)

In the above photograph is the Alva United Methodist Church, erected in 1903, while the library just up Pearl Street was built in 1909. Though the Methodist church is still an active congregation, the decision was made to move the Alva Library to the local high school in 1939. The original library building is now home to the Alva Museum. Retaining their idyllic charm of yesterday, both buildings remain in their original locations. Extensive foliage now commands this view of these buildings. (Photograph courtesy of Southwest Florida Museum of History.)

This 1914 photograph of the Captiva-Buck Key Schoolhouse captures teacher Nell Gould with her young students. The one-room schoolhouse was built on land near the Captiva Cemetery, donated by Captiva's first settler, William Herbert Binder. The schoolhouse additionally served as the community church. Originally erected in 1901, the school closed in 1921 and the land and building were sold. Today the church maintains an active, seasonal congregation and is now known as Chapel by the Sea. (Photograph courtesy of Southwest Florida Museum of History.)

Pictured above, Fort Myers School was erected at the corner of Second and Jackson Streets in 1887, after the Fort Myers Academy was destroyed by fire. Frequent Fort Myers visitor Col. Andrew D. Gwynne expressed the need for a proper school building for local children. Although Colonel Gwynne died in 1909, his family oversaw and matched fund-raising efforts. As a result, the wood-frame building was torn down and replaced with the stately brick Gwynne Institute in 1911. (Photograph courtesy of Southwest Florida Museum of History.)

Located in the vicinity of today's modern campus of Trafalgar Elementary School, the Matlacha School was short-lived. Built in 1927 on land deeded by Joseph B. Blackley, the schoolhouse had one room and 12 students. Wilma Pierce served as its first and only teacher. In 1928, the decision was made to close the school and transfer all students to the new J. Colin English Elementary School in North Fort Myers. Cape Coral would not have its own school again until 1964. (Photograph courtesy of the Cape Coral Historical Society Museum.)

A short time after the bankruptcy of the St. James on the Gulf Company, the Sisal and Hemp Development Company set up a factory complex in St. James City. Pictured below is the schoolhouse built by the corporation in 1912. Abandoned when the company shut down its operations, the building was relocated several times. It currently serves as The Waterfront Restaurant and Marina on Oleander Street. (Photograph courtesy of Southwest Florida Museum of History.)

Today it is known as the First United Methodist Church of Bonita Springs, but in the early days of Bonita Springs, residents worshipped at Lee Memorial Methodist Church. Located on Shriver Avenue near the heart of old Bonita, the building was constructed in 1921 by Edward Agner. Although the old church remains standing today, it is used for storage. The modern sanctuary and recent additions are utilized by the current congregation. (Photograph courtesy of Southwest Florida Museum of History.)

A bursting population in 1947 caused the tiny hamlet of Fort Myers Beach to outgrow its original schoolhouse. New property was purchased on Oak Street, and a building from Bayshore was relocated onto the new site. The original school was used to house the Fort Myers Beach Women's Club. The new school officially opened in 1948, with subsequent additions made in 1955, 1962, and 1970. The Beach School is now known as Fort Myers Beach Elementary School. (Photograph courtesy of Southwest Florida Museum of History.)

Originally vast acres of cattle ranch, owner Lee Ratner decided to develop his land into a city. In 1954, he formed the Lee County Land and Title Company, Inc., and acquired more acreage. The first family moved into Lehigh Acres in 1955. As with all fledgling communities, worship was a priority. The Church of God Lehigh was erected in 1966, built by its congregation brick by brick. Today it serves as the Harvest Ministries Church of God on Lee Boulevard. (Photograph courtesy of Southwest Florida Museum of History.)

CHAPTER 3

GOVERNMENT AND MILITARY

The above photograph depicts the 75,000 acres of Buckingham Army Airfield as it appeared in 1945 or 1946. The base was established in 1942 as an Army Air Corps Flexible Gunnery Training School. At the peak of its service, Buckingham Field housed 16,000 men. (Photograph courtesy of Southwest Florida Museum of History.)

This original sketch was drawn by Capt. Richard A. Graeffe while stationed at Fort Myers during the U.S. Civil War. It depicts the remoteness of the area before settlement and illustrates the isolation early soldiers and settlers experienced here. The modern photograph above is a testament to the determination of the early settlers to persevere and establish a successful community. (Both photographs courtesy of Southwest Florida Museum of History.)

This 1930 photograph shows the last remaining fort building of the Third Seminole War and U.S. Civil War at Fort Myers. Serving as the commanding officer's quarters, its original location was the corner of First and Jackson Streets. After many renovations and numerous owners, the house was moved to its Bay Street location in 1926 to serve as Fort Myer's first public library. It was torn down in 1937. (Photograph courtesy of Southwest Florida Museum of History.)

Although an active civilian airport since 1927, it was not until the attack on Pearl Harbor on December 7, 1941, that the U.S. Army Air Force took over Page Field and established an advanced fighter training base. The first soldiers to occupy the new base arrived in March 1942 from Barksdale, Louisiana. The soldiers were sleeping in tents because the barracks were not yet completed. The view today is quite different from the palmetto-lined field of the 1940s. (Photograph courtesy of Southwest Florida Museum of History.)

The handwritten caption on the back of this snapshot identifies the Page Field building as original wartime German prison barracks. The photograph was taken from Sixth Street looking west. During World War II, it was not unheard of for German prisoners to be housed on U.S. bases. Today that area is an industrial section of Page Park in Fort Myers. (Photograph courtesy of Southwest Florida Museum of History.)

This World War II photograph shows Fire Station No. 1 at Buckingham Army Airfield. The gunnery school set up by the Army Air Corps at Buckingham Field was one of two army air bases set up in Lee County in 1942. Although the base was a self-sufficient city, with its own fire department, hospital, and movie theater, it still tremendously boosted the local economy. Today Buckingham is a part of the Tice Fire District of Lee County. (Photograph courtesy of Southwest Florida Museum of History.)

No longer standing guard on U.S. Route 41 and South Road, the Page Field Main Gate Sentry House served as the first line of defense for the World War II fighter training school at Page Field. With the allied victory in 1945, control of the field was turned back over to Lee County. During the mid-1950s, the wooden barracks were replaced with a small terminal, which was expanded in 1960. The field has seen numerous additions over the years. (Photograph courtesy of Southwest Florida Museum of History.)

Long believed to be a part of the old fort, this home was actually built by William Marion Hendry in 1875. It was one of the oldest buildings in Fort Myers. Located on Bay Street next to the Arcade Theatre, the site is now occupied by the parking lot of a law firm. Ironically William Marion Hendy served as a member of the Confederate Cattle Guard, which unsuccessfully tried to attack Fort Myers during the Civil War. (Photograph courtesy of Southwest Florida Historical Society.)

The modest wooden courthouse had served Lee County well since it opened its doors in 1894. By 1914, the structure was considered outdated and unsanitary. Efforts made by county commissioners to erect a new, modern courthouse were repeatedly thwarted by judicial injunctions filed by local businessmen and attorneys who felt a new courthouse was unnecessary. County commissioners finally took matters into their own hands and had the old courthouse torn down. The wood was recycled into the original Lee Memorial Hospital and the new courthouse still serves Lee County today. (Photograph courtesy of Southwest Florida Museum of History.)

Erected in 1949 by the Florida Forestry Service, the Cape Coral Fire Tower stood watch from the southeast corner of Pine Island Road and Chiquita Boulevard until 1972. From 1949 until 1952, forestry service rangers stood watch on the tower. During 1952 to 1954, Martha Moulter manned the tower, followed by Martha's mother, Ida, from 1954 until it was disassembled in 1972. The field is now lined with residential homes. (Photograph courtesy of the Cape Coral Historical Society Museum.)

When the original Pineland Post Office was destroyed by a storm in 1925, resident Ruby Gill took action and rebuilt it on her own property in a protected location. Over the years, the U.S. Postal Service has tried to deactivate the Pineland office and merge it with Bokeelia's post office; however, Pineland's residents, proud of their heritage, always fight this effort. Lee County currently owns the property and leases it to the U.S. Postal Service. (Photograph courtesy of Southwest Florida Museum of History.)

The above building was originally constructed in 1927 as part of the Fort Myers Pleasure Pier near the Caloosahatchee Bridge. In 1943, the pilings of the pier were deemed unsafe. The building was then barged to its present location at Edwards Drive and Hendry Street, where it served as a World War II USO for U.S. servicemen, as well as other civic functions. The worn building still stands as a silent reminder of the U.S. soldiers who bravely fought more than 65 years ago. (Photograph courtesy of Southwest Florida Museum of History.)

According to old diagrams of Buckingham Field, the base's administrative offices, such as the below quartermaster's office, were located around what is now a residential area known as Buckingham Airpark. Today those homes include hangars for residents' private aircraft. Street signs and stop signs are located at ground level so as not to clip wingtips, and cars must yield to aircraft. In addition to private aircraft, the old airbase is utilized by Lee County Mosquito Control. (Photograph courtesy of Southwest Florida Museum of History.)

While passing Page Field in Fort Myers along U.S. Route 41, it is a common sight to witness aircraft takeoffs and landings right over one's vehicle. With the area now considered a commercial mecca, it is hard to imagine a time when fighter aircraft charged along those same runways training their pilots for war. The below photograph, taken in 1944, follows the landing of a B-24 Liberator. (Photograph courtesy of Southwest Florida Museum of History.)

CHAPTER 4

BUSINESS AND INDUSTRY

In the late 1880s, phosphate was discovered just northeast of Boca Grande. As a result, extensive mining and shipping networks for the mineral were set up at the port. This is a 1950s image of the phosphate docks at Port Boca Grande. Removal of the docks began in the 1990s; however, some pilings are still visible today. (Photograph courtesy of Southwest Florida Historical Society.

This photograph dating from 1900 is of a sawmill standing where Whiskey Creek intersects McGregor Boulevard. The secret moonshine still, run by William Clay, is what gave the famous creek its name. Local residents, as well as traveling cattlemen and Seminoles, were all faithful customers. Today the area is a thriving upscale community, a far cry from the rumrunners who used Whiskey Creek to cover their clandestine activities. (Photograph courtesy of Southwest Florida Historical Society.)

The original Blind Pass Bridge separating Sanibel Island from Captiva Island was built in 1918 by J. P. Loftin. This photograph is most likely of the second bridge, built sometime after 1921. Over the years, the shifting sands have slowly filled in the pass until it is bone dry. The channel has been dredged several times throughout the years, most recently in 2009. The pass now flows again under the modern concrete Blind Pass Bridge, which replaced the wooden bridge in 1954. (Photograph courtesy of Southwest Florida Museum of History.)

In this 1898 photograph of the Boca Grande Lighthouse, erected in 1890, is Capt. Peter Nelson posing on the steps. Captain Nelson was the founder of Alva, and later in life, he became a harbor pilot at Port Boca Grande. The lighthouse, automated in 1956, was destined for deactivation in 1966. It was placed on the National Register of Historic Places in 1980. The light station was eventually restored, recommissioned by the Coast Guard, and now operates as the Boca Grande Lighthouse Museum, allowing public access. (Photograph courtesy of Southwest Florida Museum of History.)

Palm trees now line the path of the long ago dock where early Fort Myers bustled with activity. In the early 1900s, George F. Ireland sold his hardware business and tried his hand in the oil business. As a distributor for the Gulf Refining Company, Ireland built warehouses and tanks at the old Blount Wharf at the foot of Hendry Street. This wharf would eventually grow and become known as Ireland Dock. (Photograph courtesy of Southwest Florida Museum of History.)

Although the first settlement on Sanibel Island during 1833 was abandoned around 1836, subsequent attempts by homesteaders were successful. This 1910 photograph of Periwinkle Road on Sanibel depicts the rugged conditions and isolation the island's first settlers had to contend with. Still retaining much of its historic foliage today, the road itself is now lined with paved bike paths, chic upscale shops, and luxurious hotels and condominiums. (Photograph courtesy of Southwest Florida Museum of History.)

At the intersection of Slater Road and Interstate 75 stood the long-gone community of Slater. In 1924, the J. W. McWilliams Company developed a lumber enterprise. In 1929, McWilliams sold the entire operation to Dowling and Camp, Inc. When the area was logged out, the tracks were simply picked up and moved to next location. After the entire region was timbered out in 1944, Dowling and Camp ceased their operations at Slater. No evidence except for the old rail beds exists there today. (Photograph courtesy of Southwest Florida Museum of History.)

Dr. Franklin Miles, founder of Miles Laboratories, was another prominent Fort Myers visitor, whose stay became permanent in 1908. Pictured below, the Miles family "in-town" residence was located on First Street near Park Avenue at the foot of today's Edison Bridge. The Miles estate, also known as the Shell House, was located where the Cape Coral Bridge enters Fort Myers. The Miles family was spared when the Shell House was destroyed by fire in 1926. At the time, the family was staying at their First Street residence. (Photograph courtesy of Southwest Florida Museum of History.)

This photograph of the Carson Street Dock was taken around 1925. Formerly the dock of the Fort Myers Steamship Company, by that time it was owned by Baron Collier's Florida Railroad and Navigation Company. The wharf also went by the name of Collier Terminal. At that time, the Fort Myers waterfront began at Bay Street. Over the years, the land was eventually filled in. Today a rest pavilion at Centennial Park stands approximately where the dock stood over the Caloosahatchee. (Photograph courtesy of Southwest Florida Museum of History.)

It was decided in the early 1920s that a road was needed heading north out of Fort Myers. Heated debates ensued over where to build that road, as the choice was to add an extension link in either the Dixie Highway to Arcadia or in the Tamiami Trail to Punta Gorda. Eventually the link in the Dixie Highway commenced construction in 1922 from Olga to Arcadia. Today the road is a heavily commuted portion of Highway 31 in Olga. (Photograph courtesy of the Southwest Florida Historical Society.)

Although palm trees have replaced the power poles, the power station at old Port Boca Grande still retains its architectural heritage. It now serves as the sales office and community center for a housing development. The power station was built in 1909 by the American Agricultural Chemical Company and was used to power all of Boca Grande. The plant was shut down in 1952 when Florida Power and Light was awarded the contract to power Gasparilla Island. (Photograph courtesy of Southwest Florida Museum of History.)

Pictured below is the original Fort Myers lab of inventor Thomas Edison. Edison's friend, Henry Ford, insisted the lab be moved to Ford's museum in Michigan. Edison agreed; however, workers were required to dig up the dirt from under the lab as Edison stipulated the lab must remain on Florida soil. Above is the lab, built in 1928 for the Edison Botanic Research Corporation—a joint venture of Edison, Ford, and Harvey Firestone. (Photograph courtesy of Southwest Florida Museum of History.)

The Atlantic Coast Line Railroad had serviced Fort Myers since 1904. But it was during the land boom of the 1920s when the decision was made that Fort Myers needed to replace the old wooden depot with a modern one. The new Spanish-style railway building opened to residents and businesses in 1924. As progressive modes of transportation evolved, railroad interests were hit hard; as a result, the Atlantic Coast Line pulled out of Fort Myers in 1971. (Photograph courtesy of Southwest Florida Museum of History.

When it first opened its doors in 1965, Lehigh Acres General Hospital was the pride of the community. The hospital originally had 50 beds, 50 extended care units, and expansive plans for future growth. In 1983, the older building was replaced with a modern state-of-the-art facility. In 2001, the hospital joined the Health Management Associates, Inc., network. Along with the change in ownership came a new name: Lehigh Regional Medical Center, as it is still known today. (Photograph courtesy of Southwest Florida Museum of History.)

Around 1935, a new flower was discovered to thrive in the fertile soil and temperate climate of Fort Myers. The three major growers of gladiolus all set up operations in the Iona district of Fort Myers. The pictured gladiolus field was at the intersection of Summerlin and Winkler Roads. At one point, more gladioli grew in the Iona district of Fort Myers than in any other location in the United States. (Photograph courtesy of Southwest Florida Museum of History.)

With the remoteness of the surrounding barrier islands, seaplane service became popular throughout Lee County. With the complaints of noisy aircraft tying up at the foot of the Edison Bridge or at the city pier, the county board of commissioners finally agreed to the construction of a seaplane base in the late 1930s. Gulf Airways delivered newspapers, offered sightseeing trips, or provided commutes from their base in the vicinity of North Shore Drive in North Fort Myers. (Photograph courtesy of Southwest Florida Museum of History.)

With the population boom of Lee County in the late 1950s and early 1960s, extreme stress was being placed on Lee County's natural resources and waterways. The Army Corps of Engineers set to work in 1962 on the W. P. Franklin Lock and Dam. Originally named the Olga Lock, the facility officially opened in 1965 and is still in use. Today the W. P. Franklin Lock and Dam Recreational Area consists of a camping ground and a beach and park on the Caloosahatchee. (Photograph courtesy of Southwest Florida Historical Society.)

Located in the vicinity of St. Andrew's Church, the Cape Coral Airport was built in 1962. The airport was initially only to be used by Gulf American Land Corporation for their sales flights; however, local pilots and eventually some commercial flights utilized the small airport. In 1965, Gulf American moved their air operations to Page Field. Today the land west of Del Prado near Everest is a quiet residential section of Cape Coral. (Photograph courtesy of Cape Coral Historical Society Museum.)

CHAPTER 5

RECREATION

Built in 1886, Battery Wharf served as the dock of St. James City's famed Hotel San Carlos. The road from the dock angled up Palm Avenue directly onto the hotel grounds. It extended 600 feet into the bay, and then made a right angle for several hundred more feet into the general store. The wharf was sold when the hotel burned down in 1905. (Photograph courtesy of Southwest Florida Historical Society.)

The jewel of St. James City was the Hotel San Carlos. Built in 1886 by the St. James on the Gulf Company, the upscale resort welcomed guests such as Thomas Edison, Henry Ford, and Sam Colt. Due to bankruptcy, the hotel, lands, and wharf were auctioned off in the early 1900s. A fire in 1905 swept through the area, burning the hotel to the ground. Today the landmark site is a private, residential mobile home park. (Photograph courtesy of Southwest Florida Museum of History.)

Now a barren field in Alva, one can almost still hear the clatter of hooves and the banter of the early patrons of the Hotel Three Oaks. The hotel first opened its doors in 1903. The original owner, Henry A. Lee, who also served as the Alva Bridge tender, named his establishment for the three oak trees he planted near his hotel. The hotel was located near the river at Pearl Street and Broadway Street. (Photograph courtesy of Southwest Florida Museum of History.)

When the International Ocean and Telegraph Company took over the old army barracks at Punta Rassa, the telegrapher stationed there, George Schultz, quickly saw that he could provide meals and shelter to the visiting cowboys. As the cattle trade decreased, Schultz converted the barracks into a sportsman's lodge named Tarpon House. When Tarpon House burned in 1906, the lodge was rebuilt with the financing of its wealthy patrons. Fire struck the lodge again in 1913, but this time it was never reconstructed. (Photograph courtesy of Southwest Florida Museum of History.)

This 1910 photograph of the Fort Myers Beach Pier shows the rustic origins of the structure. Changing ownership many times throughout the years, the pier also suffered damaged from the severe southwest Florida weather. In 1975, the pier was condemned and closed to the public, a new concrete pier was constructed a year later. Today restaurants and shops line the foot of the busy pier. (Photograph courtesy of Southwest Florida Museum of History.)

Made of coquina rock, the Fort Myers Beach arches were built in 1924 by developer Tom Phillips. The arches were located at the entrance to the beach at San Carlos Boulevard. The historic landmark was demolished to make way for the new high-rise bridge at Matanzas Pass, built in the mid-1970s. An attempt to either save or move the arches was unsuccessful. Now waterfront restaurants at Fisherman's Wharf occupy the land where the Fort Myers Beach arches once stood. (Photograph courtesy of Southwest Florida Museum of History.)

Located at what is now the intersection of Bay Street and Royal Palm Avenue, the Royal Palm Hotel was built in 1898 by Hugh O'Neill. Originally the hotel was named the Fort Myers Hotel. O'Neill revitalized the landscaping, planting hundreds of royal palms, as well as other tropical plants and shrubbery, inspiring the hotel to rename itself. With his knack for advertising, O'Neill transformed the lodge into a prestigious winter resort for the affluent. The Royal Palm Hotel was torn down in 1948. (Photograph courtesy of Southwest Florida Museum of History.)

In 1905, Dr. Marshall Orlando Terry and his wife, Fort Myers benefactress Tootie McGregor Terry, donated 40 acres of land to Lee County for use as fairgrounds. County commissioners, having lured the Philadelphia Athletics to Fort Myers for spring training, decided Terry Park was the field of choice. In 1925, construction on a small wooden grandstand seating 600 spectators was completed. Over the years, 100 "Hall of Famers" played baseball on Terry Park's field, allowing it to be registered as a historical landmark. (Photograph courtesy of Southwest Florida Museum of History.)

When new owner Earl Wheelock purchased the Captiva Hotel, he changed the name of the establishment to the Captiva Lodge. The photograph below faces the rear of what at the time was the Captiva Hotel's complex. The popular island resort also went by the names of Bayview Hotel and Fisherman's Lodge. The building was destroyed by fire in 1948. (Photograph courtesy of Southwest Florida Museum of History.)

Doc Baird's Tourist Camp was a conglomerate of tourist cottages and tent sites for travelers through the area. What made the camp famous was its honky-tonk tavern with its wild reputation. Built by Ruth and Archer "Doc" Baird around 1925, the camp was located on the south side of the Imperial River, across from where the Liles Hotel stands today. Many of Bonita's leading citizens refused to frequent such an establishment; however, Doc Baird's never wanted for customers. (Photograph courtesy of Southwest Florida Museum of History.)

Now a quiet stretch of gulf coast beach at Connecticut Street, the area was once home to the Seminole Sands Casino. Opened in 1921, the complex would eventually include the casino, a hotel, café, and dance pavilion. The casino's owner, Jack DeLysle, was arrested for allegedly smuggling rum off Naples but was acquitted. On October 26, 1921, a hurricane damaged the enterprise, but DeLysle rebuilt. In 1924, a beachside bonfire sparked a blaze and burned the complex to the ground. (Photograph courtesy of Southwest Florida Museum of History.)

Fisherman's Lodge was originally known as the Bayview Hotel. It would also eventually be known as the Captiva Hotel and the Captiva Lodge. The hotel was built in stages by original owner F. A. Lane of Hartford, Connecticut. In 1911, construction began at what is now a residential section of Captiva located at Old Lodge Lane and Binder Drive and was not completed until 1915. A popular fishing resort, the lodge remained closed for many years following Lane's sudden death. (Photograph courtesy of Southwest Florida Museum of History.)

On January 1, 1937, work began on what would become a Fort Myers institution. The Yacht Basin was a Works Progress Administration project, under Franklin D. Roosevelt's New Deal program. The Great Depression hit Lee County hard, and the Yacht Basin was able to provide many job opportunities for the unemployed of Fort Myers. The project took approximately two years to complete. Today the Yacht Basin is one of the most popular recreation areas in Fort Myers, providing facilities for boating enthusiasts and landlubbers alike. (Photograph courtesy of Southwest Florida Museum of History.)

The north end of Fort Myers beach is still the quiet area of town. While most homesteaders and business owners chose the middle or southern portions of Estero Island to settle, the isle's northern end seemed to attract homeowners looking for the tranquility of a quiet beach home, as shown in this 1945 photograph. Today modern high-rise condominiums have taken over the north end of Fort Myers Beach; however, the area still remains free of local business establishments. (Photograph courtesy of Southwest Florida Museum of History.)

Cape Coral's Iwo Jima Memorial statue was constructed by Felix de Weldon, the artist behind the Iwo Jima Memorial in Washington. The statue first graced the entrance to the Cape Coral Wonder Gardens, located near today's Rotary Park, in 1964. After the gardens closed, the statue was vandalized and left to deteriorate. Restored by de Weldon, the statue was moved to North First Bank, then to Nations Bank. In 1997, the statue was moved to its present location on Veterans Parkway near the Midpoint Bridge. (Photograph courtesy of the Cape Coral Historical Society Museum.)

This photograph of Sanibel Island's famed CasaYbel Resort dates to 1972. The island's first hotel, it was built approximately 1890 by the father of Marie and Georgia Barnes of Kentucky and was appropriately christened The Sisters. When the resort changed ownership in 1900, the name officially changed to the CasaYbel Resort, as it remains today. Catering to patrons such as Thomas Edison and Charles Lindbergh, the resort has undergone numerous renovations over time, yet still remains a favorite of travelers seeking the serenity of Sanibel Island. (Photograph courtesy of Southwest Florida Museum of History.)

Cape Coral's first business establishment opened its doors in 1959. The Surfside Restaurant, located on Cape Coral Parkway, was built by Gulf American Land Corporation to provide amenities to Cape Coral's residents and impress potential home buyers. The Surfside served as the general store, post office, and community center. The restaurant survived fire, Hurricane Donna, and the filming of the television series *Route 66*. Gulf American sold the restaurant in 1971. No longer standing, another restaurant now occupies its site. (Photograph courtesy of Cape Coral Historical Society Museum.)

When they opened their doors in 1936, brothers Lester and Bill Piper originally called their wildlife exhibit the Everglades Reptile Gardens. By the late 1940s, they dropped the word "reptile," feeling it scared off potential customers and changed the name to the Everglades Wonder Gardens. Considered early environmentalists, the Pipers would accept and rehabilitate orphaned or injured wildlife, and they ran a successful breeding program for panthers. Today the long-standing Bonita Springs institution is owned by David Piper Jr., grandson of Lester Piper. (Photograph courtesy of Southwest Florida Museum of History.)

Built in the early 1940s, the outside of Bonita Spring's Dome Restaurant was covered with coral rock, and the dome-shaped roof was painted an appropriate bright orange color, topped with a green leaf. After the Shell Factory burned down in 1952, the local economy, including the Dome Restaurant, was devastated. Eventually the diner turned into a tavern. The Dome Restaurant was torn down in 1992. The original site on the northeast corner of Terry Street and Old U.S. Route 41 is now a gas station. (Photograph courtesy of Southwest Florida Historical Society.)

Originally built in the early 1960s by Gulf American Land Corporation for use as their sales office, the Rotunda Building was donated to the city of Cape Coral for use as a library. Gulf American also paid for the relocation of the building to its present site, installation of water and sanitation facilities, and landscaping. With a booming population, the library quickly outgrew its new facility and moved elsewhere in the early 1970s. Today the building houses the Cape Coral Arts Studio. (Photograph courtesy of the Cape Coral Historical Society Museum.)

Pictured below around 1935 is the original banyan tree outside the Lee County Courthouse. The current photograph does not do the expansive growth of the tree justice. A recent war waged concerning the original oak tree outside of the courthouse, which some deemed dangerous. Once properly documented by preservation groups, the oak tree will be removed. Today the banyan tree continues growing where it was planted over 100 years ago. (Photograph courtesy of Southwest Florida Museum of History.)

MAP SEARCH